DÀODĚJĪNG

老子道德經

Translated by

M. Joseph Walden

DAODEJING

Copyright © 2012 M. Joseph Walden

All rights reserved

ISBN 978-1-105-73610-0

Book I

THE BOOK OF THE WAY

道經

.1.

Dào can be conveyed,
道 可 道

But not unchanging dào.
非 常 道

Names can be attributed,
名 可 名

But not unchanging names.
非 常 名

The origin of heaven and earth is nameless,
無 名 天 地 之 始

Yet we may call her "mother of everything."
有名萬物之母

This is why, when one trusts in her sufficiency,
故常無欲[1]

Dào inspires awe;
以觀其妙

When one fears deficiency,
常有欲也

Her outer fringes remain manifest.
以觀其徼

These two arise as one—
兩者同出

Differing in name, sharing one center.
異名同胃

Mystery of all mysteries,
玄之又玄

The gate to awe.
衆妙之門

.2.

When everyone knows
天 下 皆 知

Beauty as being beautiful,
美 之 為 美

This only makes their hearts ugly.
此 斯 惡2 已

When everyone knows
天 下 皆 知

Good as doing good,
善 之 為 善

This cannot be good.
斯 不 善 已

Non-being and being give birth to each other,
有 無 相 生

Difficult and easy complete each other,
難 易 相 成

Long and short reveal each other,
長 短 相 較

High and low measure each other,
高下相傾

Melody and harmony satisfy each other,
音聲相和

Before and after follow each other.
前後相隨

The wise ones
是以聖人

Earn their livelihood with non-action,
居無為之事

Following wordless teachings.
行不言之教

All things arise,
萬物作

And they do not speak against them,
而不辭

Allowing them to grow without possessing them.
生而不有

They do their work, but expect no reward;
為 而 不 恃

They accomplished their task, and move on.
成 而 弗 居

It is precisely because they move on
夫 唯 弗 居

That they never depart.
是 以 不 去

.3.

Not honoring the talented,
不 尚 賢

The people cease striving against nature.
使 民 不 爭[3]

Not prizing unattainable goods,
不 貴 難 得 之 貨

The people cease stealing.
使 民 不 為 盜

Not displaying what is desirable,
不 見 可 欲

The people's minds are undisturbed.
使 民 心 不 亂

The rule of the wise ones is this:
是 以 聖 人 之 治

Empty the mind, fill the belly;
虛 其 心 實 其 腹

Relax the ambitions, toughen the bones.
弱 其 志 強 其 骨

This leads people away from learnedness and want,
常 使 民 無 知[4] 無 欲

And keeps the clever ones from daring to meddle.
使 夫 智 者 不 敢 為 也

Act without action,
為 無 為

And this rule brings order to everything.
則 無 不 治

.4.

Pour dào out,
道 沖

And she cannot be depleted;
而 用 之 或 不 盈

So deep—
淵 兮

She seems to be the ancestor of everything.
似 萬 物 之 宗

So still—
湛 兮

She seems to endure forever.
似 或 存

I do not know whose child she is;
吾 不 知 誰 之 子

She is the origin of every archetype.
象 帝 之 先[5]

.5.

Heaven and earth cater to no one—
天 地 不 仁[6]

They treat everyone
以 萬 物 為

Impartially.
芻 狗[7]

The wise ones cater to no one—
聖 人 不 仁

They treat everyone
以 百 姓 為

Impartially.
芻 狗

The space between heaven and earth:
天 地 之 間

How it is like a bellows—
其 猶 橐 籥 乎

Empty, yet inexhaustible!
虛 而 不 屈

Draw upon it, and still it gives ever more.
動 而 愈 出

The more words we utter, the more we wither;
多 言 數 窮

Unless we keep watch at the center.
不 如 守 中

.6.

The spirit of the valley never dies,
谷 神 不 死

It is called the mysterious womb.
是 謂 玄 牝[8]

The mysterious womb's opening
玄 牝 之 門

Is called the root of heaven and earth.
謂 天 地 根

Saturating everything, yet barely seeming,
系 系[9] 若 存

It realizes its purpose without toil.
用[10] 之 不 勤

.7.

Heaven is everlasting, and earth is ancient.
天 長 地 久

The reason that heaven and earth
天 地 所 以

Are able to last so long
能 長 且 久

Is that they do not live for themselves;
以 其 不 自 生

And so, they are able to live forever.
故 能 長 生

The wise ones
是 以 聖 人

Remain behind,
後 其 身

But find themselves in front.
而 身 先

They reject themselves,
外 其 身

Yet they are preserved.
而 身 存

They are without "self"—
不 以 其 無 私 輿

By this, "self" is realized.
故 能 成 其 私

.8.

The highest good is like water:
上 善 若 水

Water benefits everything without striving.
水 善 利 萬 物 而 不 爭

It stays in places that society despises:
處 眾 人 之 所 惡

Here, reverently, it approaches dào.
故 幾 於 道

It is good to dwell on solid ground.
居 善 地

It is good to reflect deeply.
心 善 淵

It is good to treat others kindly.
與 善 仁 [6]

It is good to speak sincerely.
言 善 信

It is good to govern justly.
政 善 治

It is good to work efficiently.
事 善 能

It is good to act unhesitantly.
動 善 時

Above all, not striving against nature,
夫 唯 不 爭 [3]

One is free from fault.
故 無 尤

.9.

Taking when there is enough—
持 而 盈 之

It is better to stop.
不 如 其 已

Sharpening and beating a sword—
揣 而 銳 之

It cannot be preserved for long.
不 可 長 保

Filling the halls with gold and jade—
金 玉 滿 堂

It cannot be guarded.
莫 能 守 也

Taking pride in riches and honor—
富 貴 而 驕

What follows is downfall.
自 遺 其 咎

When the work is finished, retire—
功 遂 身 退

This is the way of heaven.
天 之 道 也

.10.

Bearing mind and life together as one,
載 營 魄 抱 一

It is possible to see beyond distinctions!
能 無 離 乎

Gently attending to one's vital force
專 氣[11] 致 柔

It is possible to be innocent as a child!
能 嬰 兒 乎

Cleaning and polishing the vision of mystery,
滌 除 玄 鑒

It is possible to be unobscured!
能 如 疵 乎

Loving the nation and leading society,
愛 國 治 民

It is possible to be without action!
能 無 為 乎

While taking in sights and sounds,
天 門 開 闔[12]

One can remain tranquil as a mother bird!
能 為 雌 乎 13

Shining and pure, peering into all directions,
明 白 四 達

It is possible to let go of learnedness!
能 無 知 4 乎

Growing, cultivating;
生 之 畜 之

Growing, but not possessing;
生 而 不 有

Working, but expecting no reward;
為 而 不 恃

Leading, but not controlling;
長 而 不 宰

This is called profound virtue.
是 謂 玄 德

.11.

Thirty spokes share a single hub,
三 十 輻 共 一 轂

Because of the emptiness at its center,
當 其 無

The wheel has a purpose.
有 車 之 用 [10]

We make a vessel by shaping clay,
埏 埴 以 為 器

Because of the emptiness at the center,
當 其 無

The vessel has a purpose.
有 器 之 用

We cut doors and windows for a house,
鑿 戶 牖 以 為 室

Because of the emptiness at the center,
當 其 無

The home has a purpose.
有 室 之 用

Being makes things profitable,
故 有 之 以 為 利

But emptiness gives it purpose.
無 之 以 為 用

.12.

The five colors blind the eye.
五 色 令 人 目 盲

The five tones deafen the ear.
五 音 令 人 耳 聾

The five flavors destroy the palate.
五 味 令 人 口 爽

Racing and hunting madden the mind.
馳 騁 畋 獵 令 人 心 發 狂

Difficult to obtain goods limit our actions.
難 得 之 貨 令 人 行 妨

The wise ones act from within, not from their eyes.
是 以 聖 人 為 腹 不 為 目

They reject the latter to receive the former.
故 去 彼 取 此

.13.

Struggling with honors and disgraces causes anxiety.
寵 辱 若 驚

Attachment to an unchangeable identity is anguish.
貴 大 患 若 身[14]

What does it mean to say:
何 謂

Struggling with honors and disgraces causes anxiety?
寵 辱 若 驚

Honor casts one down;
寵 為 下

Gaining rank makes one anxious.
得 之 若 驚

Losing rank makes one anxious.
失 之 若 驚

This is what it means to say:
是 謂

Struggling with honors and disgraces causes anxiety.
寵 辱 若 驚

What does this mean:
何 謂

Attachment to an unchangeable identity is anguish?
貴 大 患 若 身

The reason I suffer so greatly
吾 所 以 有 大 患 者

Is that I am attached to an idea of self.
為 吾 有 身

I was once without a self;
及 吾 無 身

Now what trouble I bear!
吾 有 何 患

One who sacrifices "self" for the world
故 貴 以 身 為 天 下

May be entrusted with the world.
若 可 寄 天 下

One who is willing to renounce "self" for the world
愛 以 身 為 天 下

May be the guardian of the world.
若 可 托 天 下

.14.

What is not seen is called invisible.
視 之 不 見 名 曰 夷

What is not heard is called inaudible.
聽 之 不 聞 名 曰 希

What is not touched is called incorporeal.
搏 之 不 得 名 曰 微

These three cannot be further investigated,
此 三 者 不 可 致 詰

And so they blend and become one.
故 混 而 為 一

Above it is not bright, below it is not dark.
其 上 不 皦 其 下 不 昧

Boundless, boundless and unnameable,
繩 繩 不 可 名

It is elusive, and returns to nothingness.
復 歸 於 無 物

This is called formless form,
是 狀 無 狀

Imageless image;
無象之象

This is called indefinable and unimaginable.
是謂惚恍

Stand before it, and its face cannot be seen.
迎之不見其首

Follow behind it, its back cannot be seen.
隨之不見其後

But abide in the ancient dào,
執古之道

And the present is mastered.
以御今之有

Then the origin is known;
能知古始

This is called inheriting dào.
是謂道紀

.15.

In ancient times,
古之

The best practitioners
善為道者

Were subtly mysterious and deeply penetrating;
微妙玄通

Too deep to understand.
深不可識

Because they cannot be understood,
夫唯不可識

It takes a strong effort to describe them:
故強為之容

Cautious! Like crossing a frozen stream in the winter,
豫兮若冬涉川

Vigilant! Like one fearing danger on all sides,
猶兮若畏四鄰

Reserved! Like a visiting stranger,
儼兮其若客

Yielding! Like ice about to melt,
渙兮若冰將釋

Genuine! Like natural simplicity,
敦兮其若樸[15]

Open! Like a valley,
曠兮其若谷

Chaotic! Like muddied waters.
混兮其若濁

Calm! Like the sea,
澹兮其若海

Brutal! As though never-ending.
飂兮若無止

By keeping still, the muddied slowly becomes clear.
孰能濁以靜之徐清

By constant motion, life in the womb slowly grows.
孰能安以動之徐生

One who embraces dào does not want to overflow;
保此道者不欲盈

It is precisely because they do not want to overflow
夫 唯 不 欲 盈

That they may wear on without ever needing rest.
故 能 蔽 而 新 成

.16.

Attain complete emptiness—
致 虛 極

Abide in the still depths.
守 靜 篤

Everything arises together:
萬 物 并 作

In this I see their cyclical nature.
吾 以 觀 復[16]

All things flourish, flourish,
夫 物 芸 芸

Each returning to its root.
各 復 歸 其 根

Returning to the root is called stillness.
歸 根 曰 靜

Stillness is called the cycle of nature.
靜 曰 復 命

The cycle of nature is called unchanging.
復 命 曰 常

Knowing the unchanging is called enlightenment.
知 常 曰 明

Not knowing the unchanging brings about disaster;
不 知 常 妄 作 兇

Knowing the unchanging, one embraces all.
知 常 容

To be all-embracing is to be impartial.
容 乃 公

To be impartial is to be perfected.
公 乃 全

To be perfected is to be heavenly,
全 乃 天

To be heavenly is to be of the dào,
天 乃 道

Dào is immortal.
道 乃 久

Leave prone the concept of "self;" be free of danger.
沒 身 不 殆[17]

.17.

Great leaders are not noticed by their people.
太 上 不 知 有 之

The next best are cherished and praised by them.
其 次 親 而 譽 之

The next best are feared by them.
其 次 畏 之

The next best are despised by them.
其 次 侮 之

Without trusting others,
信 不 足 焉

One will not be trusted.
有 不 信 焉

Quiet! Why treasure words?
悠 兮 其 貴 言 [18]

When one does things well,
功 成 事 遂

People will say it happened on its own
百 姓 皆 謂 我 自 然 [19]

.18.

When the great dào is abandoned,
大 道 廢

Then there is philanthropy and justice,
有 仁 [6] 義

Wittiness and cleverness arise;
慧 智 出

There is great hypocrisy;
有 大 偽

Communities fail to cooperate;
六 親 不 和

Compassion is reduced to obeisance,
有 孝 慈

National policy is disordered and confused,
國 家 昏 亂

And the subjects become nationalistic.
有 忠 臣

.19.

Abandon self-righteousness and discard cleverness
絶 聖[20] 棄 智

And the people will benefit one-hundredfold.
民 利 百 倍

Abandon philanthropy and discard justice
絶 仁[6] 棄 義

And the people will return to compassion.
民 復 孝 慈

Abandon cleverness and discard profit,
絶 巧 棄 利

Then thieves and robbers will disappear.
盜 賊 無 有

These three things are superficial and insufficient—
此 三 者 以 為 文 不 足

Master them or be mastered by them;
或 令 之 或 所 屬

Recognize plainness and nourish natural simplicity,
視 素 保 樸 [15]

39

Reduce the ego, diminish attachments.
少私寡欲

Abandon learnedness and there will be no sorrow.
絕學無憂

.20.

"Yes" is the contrary of "no";
唯 之 與 阿

How little is the difference between them?
相 去 幾 何

"Good" is the contrary of "evil";
善 之 與 惡

How much are they alike?
相 去 若 何

One who is feared
人 之 所 畏

Must fear others;
不 可 不 畏

This untamed wilderness has no end!
荒 兮 其 未 央 哉

Society is joyful, joyful—
衆 人 熙 熙

Like they are feasting on a fat ox,
如 享 太 牢

As if taking in the sights of springtime.
如 春 登 臺

I alone remain calm, showing no sign,
我 獨 泊 兮 其 未 兆

Like a newborn child who has not yet smiled.
如 嬰 兒 之 未 孩

Weary, weary as one without a home.
儽 儽 兮 若 無 所 歸

Society has abundance, but I alone seem lacking.
衆 人 皆 有 餘 而 我 獨 若 遺

My mind is like a fool's—confused, confused!
我 愚 人 之 心 也 哉 沌 沌 兮

The common people are brilliant, brilliant;
俗 人 昭 昭

I alone am dim, dim.
我 獨 昏 昏

The common people are sharp, sharp;
俗 人 察 察

I alone am dull, dull.
我獨悶悶

They are like the tranquil ocean;
澹兮其若海

I am like an unceasing whirlwind.
飂兮若無止

Society has a purpose,
衆人皆有以

But I alone am awkward and unrefined.
而我獨頑且鄙

I alone differ
我獨異於人

Because I receive nourishment from my mother.
而貴食母

.21.

Practicing all-embracing virtue
孔 德 之 容

Comes only from dào.
惟 道 是 從

But dào's actions
道 之 為 物

Are vague and elusive.
惟 恍 惟 惚

Elusive and vague,
惚 兮 恍 兮

Within is contained an image.
其 中 有 象

Vague and elusive,
恍 兮 惚 兮

Within is contained an object.
其 中 有 物

Hidden and obscure,
窈 兮 冥 兮

Within is contained meaning.
其 中 有 精

This meaning is very real;
其 精 甚 真

Within is contained truth.
其 中 有 信

From antiquity until now,
自 今 及 古

Her name has not departed.
其 名 不 去

By this, the origin of everything is revealed;
以 閱 衆 甫

By stopping and sitting, I can know all beginnings.
吾 何 以 知 衆 甫 之 狀 哉 以 此[21]

.22.

Surrender and become perfect.
曲 則 全

Be crooked and become rectified.
枉 則 直

Be empty and become filled.
窪 則 盈

Be worn out and become renewed.
敝 則 新

Have little and receive.
少 則 得

Have much and become bewildered.
多 則 惑

The wise ones embrace oneness
是 以 聖 人 抱 一

And become the measure of the world.
為 天 下 式

They are not occupied by themselves, so they shine,
不 自 見 故 明

Do not assert themselves, so they are recognized,
不 自 是 故 彰

Do not boast about themselves, so they merit,
不 自 伐 故 有 功

Do not make a show of themselves, so they endure.
不 自 矜 故 長

Precisely because they do not strive against nature,
夫 唯 不 爭 [3]

So nothing in the world can strive against them.
故 天 下 莫 能 與 之 爭

The ancients said:
古 之 所 謂

Surrender and become perfect.
曲 則 全

These are not empty words:
豈 虛 言 哉

True perfection is achieved through turning back.
誠 全 而 歸 之

.23.

Nature is of few words:
希 言 自 然 [19]

A strong wind does not last all morning,
故 飄 風 不 終 朝

A violent storm does not outlast a day.
驟 雨 不 終 日

Why is this so? Heaven and earth make it so.
孰 為 此 者 天 地

Heaven and earth do not sustain anything forever,
天 地 尚 不 能 久

Much less humanity!
而 況 於 人 乎

One decides their devotions daily.
故 從 事 於

The devotee of dào is allied with dào.
道 者 同 於 道

The devotee of dào's virtue is allied with virtue.
德 者 同 於 德 [22]

To abandon devotion is to become allied with loss.
失者同於失

Allies of dào—
同於道者

Dào is glad to welcome them.
道亦樂得之

Allies of dào's virtue—
同於德者

Virtue is glad to welcome them.
德亦樂得之

Allies of loss—
同於失者

Loss is glad to welcome them.
失亦樂得之

.24.

On tiptoes, one cannot remain standing.
企 者 不 立

Straddling, one cannot go far.
跨 者 不 行

Occupied with one's self, one cannot shine.
自 見 者 不 明

Asserting one's self, one cannot be recognized.
自 是 者 不 彰

Boasting of one's self, one is without merit.
自 伐 者 無 功

Making a show of one's self, one cannot endure.
自 矜 者 不 長

From the perspective of dào,
其 在 道 也

These are like spoiled food and tumors of action,
曰 餘 食 贅 行

Which all people despise.
物 或 惡 之

Followers of dào do not dwell in these things.
故有道者不處

.25.

There was something nebulous yet complete
有 物 混 成

Preceding the birth of heaven and earth.
先 天 地 生

Tranquil! Formless!
寂 兮 寥 兮

Alone she stands without wavering.
獨 立 不 改

Always moving but never exhausted;
周 行 而 不 殆

She can be called the mother of the world.
可 以 為 天 下 母

I do not know her name,
吾 不 知 其 名

But I like to call her "dào."
字 之 曰 道

If forced to assign a name,
強 為 之 名

I would call her "great."
曰 大

"Great" means she passes beyond;
大 曰 逝

Passing beyond means she reaches far,
逝 曰 遠

Reaching far means she returns.
遠 曰 反

Dào is great, heaven is great;
故 道 大 天 大

Earth is great, and humanity is also great.
地 大 人 亦 大

In the midst of the world there are four great things,
域 中 有 四 大

And human life is one of them.
而 人 居 其 一 焉

Humanity follows the earth,
人 法 地

Earth follows heaven;
地 法 天

Heaven follows dào,
天 法 道

Dào follows her own nature.
道 法 自 然 [19]

.26.

Heaviness is the root of lightness,
重 為 輕 根

Stillness is the master of restlessness.
靜 為 躁 君

The wise ones
是 以 聖 人

Travel every day,
終 日 行

Never abandoning their baggage.
不 離 輜 重[23]

Though they live in glorious places,
雖 有 榮 觀

They remain aloof and indifferent.
燕 處 超 然

How could the master of ten thousand chariots
奈 何 萬 乘 之 主

Behave lightly before the people of the world?
而 以 身 輕 天 下

To be light is to lose one's root,
輕 則 失 根

To be restless is to lose one's master.
躁 則 失 君

.27.

A good traveler leaves neither tracks nor trace.
善行無轍跡

A good speaker is without flaw or reproach.
善言無瑕謫

A good accountant neither counts nor calculates.
善數不用籌策

A good gate has no lock,
善閉無關楗

Yet none can open it.
而不可開

A good knot needs no rope,
善結無繩約

Yet it cannot be untied.
而不可解

The wise ones are skilled at caring for people,
是以聖人常善救人

So no one is rejected;
故無棄人

They are always skilled at caring for things,
常善救物

So things are never rejected.
故無棄物

This is called practicing enlightenment.
是謂襲明

Skillful people are the teachers of unskilled people;
故善人者不善人之師

Unskilled people are a lesson for skillful people.
不善人者善人之資

One who neither values their teacher
不貴其師

Nor loves their lesson,
不愛其資

Although clever, will be greatly confused—
雖智大迷

They deny that which calls for reverence.
是謂要妙[24]

.28.

Know the masculine, abide in the feminine,
知 其 雄 守 其 雌

Become the river of the world.
為 天 下 溪

Become the river of the world,
為 天 下 溪

And dào's virtue will never depart,
常 德 [22] 不 離

Then innocence will return.
復 歸 於 嬰 兒

Know the white, abide in the black,
知 其 白 守 其 黑

Become the measure of the world.
為 天 下 式

Becoming the measure of the world
為 天 下 式

And never straying from dào's virtue,
常 德 不 忒

One returns to the infinite.
復 歸 於 無 極

Know the light, abide in the dark,
知 其 白 守 其 辱

Become the valley of the world.
為 天 下 谷

Become the valley of the world,
為 天 下 谷

And dào's virtue will be ever sufficient,
常 德 乃 足

Then nature's simplicity will return.
復 歸 於 樸 [15]

When nature's simplicity falls apart,
樸 [15] 散

The wise ones gather the pieces,
則 為 器 聖 人 用 之

Then they become the leading officials,
則 為 官 長

And great simplicity is undivided.
故 大 制 不 割[25]

.29.

Some want to unite the world by meddling with it,
將 欲 取[26] 天 下 而 為 之

But I realize this cannot succeed.
吾 見 其 不 得 已

The world is a spiritual thing;
天 下 神 器

It must not be meddled with.
不 可 為

Meddling ruins it;
為 者 敗 之

Taking hold loses it.
執 者 失 之

Some people lead, others follow.
夫 物 或 行 或 隨

Some whisper, others yell.
或 噓 或 吹

Some are strong, others are weak.
或 強 或 羸

Some destroy, others are destroyed.
或接或隳

The wise ones
是以聖人

Abandon extremes,
去甚

Abandon extravagances,
去奢

Abandon excess.
去泰

.30.

Guide the people with dào,
以 道 佐 人 主 者

Do not dominate the world with soldiers.
不 以 兵 強 天 下

Such interference can only go so far.
其 事 好 遠

Thorn bushes grow where the army is camped.
師 之 所 處 荊 棘 生 焉

The aftermath of great wars is famine.
大 軍 之 後 必 有 兇 年

The skillful ones achieve and then stop—
善 有 果 而 已

If they dare to take hold by force,
不 以 取 強

They achieve without arrogance,
果 而 勿 矜

Achieve without boasting or pride,
果 而 勿 伐 果 而 勿 驕

Achieve, regretting that force was not avoided!
果 而 不 得 已

.31.

Even an excellent soldier is a bad omen,
夫 佳 兵 者 不 祥 之

Because their tools are despised by all.
器 物 或 惡 之

One who follows dào turns away from them.
故 有 道 者 不 處

Soldiers are bad omens—
兵 者 不 祥 之

Their tools oppose those of the master philosopher.
器 非 君 子 之 器

The slaughter of multitudes of people
殺 人 之 眾

Causes lamentation and sorrow;
以 悲 哀 泣 之

Victory in war is celebrated with funerals.
戰 勝 以 喪 禮 處 之

.32.

The unchanging dào is nameless.
道 常 無 名

Her natural simplicity, though insignificant,
樸 [15] 雖 小

Cannot be ruled over.
天 下 莫 能 臣

If rulers could abide with her,
王 侯 若 能 守 之

They would be honored by all.
萬 物 將 自 賓

Heaven and earth, joined together,
天 地 相 合

Would drip sweet dew;
以 降 甘 露

The people would have no law
民 莫 之 令

And could naturally achieve harmony.
而 自 均

When systems are created, there are names—
始 制 有 名

When there are names, know it is also time to stop.
名 亦 既 有 夫 亦 將 知 止

Knowing when to stop, there is no danger.
知 止 不 殆

Dào moves in the world
譬 道 之 在 天 下

Like rivers streaming into the ocean.
猶 川 谷 之 於 江 海

.33.

Knowing others is clever,
知 人 者 智

Knowing one's self is enlightened.
自 知 者 明

Conquering others exhibits force,
勝 人 者 有 力

Conquering self is indeed powerful.
自 勝 者 強

One who knows satisfaction is rich;
知 足 者 富

One who perseveres has discipline,
強 行 者 有 志

One who knows where they are endures;
不 失 其 所 者 久

Then, even dying, one cannot perish.
死 而 不 亡 者 壽

.34.

The great dào flows! She may go in any direction.
大 道 泛 兮 其 可 左 右

All things rely upon her to grow,
萬 物 恃 之 以 生

And she never speaks against them.
而 不 辭

Her accomplishments are meritorious,
功 成

Yet she is anonymous.
而 不 名 有

She clothes and nourishes all things,
衣 養 萬 物

Yet she does not lord over them.
而 不 為 主

She may be named "Caretaker of the lowly."
可 名 於 小

Everything returns to her
萬 物 歸 焉

Because she does not lord over them.
而不為主

She may be named "Master of the great."
可名為大

One ought not make one's self great,
以其終不自為大

So that greatness may be accomplished.
故能成其大

.35.

Contemplate this daunting image,
執大象

And the whole world appears,
天下往

Revealing itself to be harmless,
往而不害

Abundant with peace and contentment!
安平太

When there is music and cake,
樂與餌

Passing strangers stop,
過客止

But dào's words are flat and without flavor!
道之出口淡乎

Her image is imperceptible;
視之不足見

Her testimony, inaudible,
聽之不足聞

Her providence, inexhaustible.
用之不足既[27]

.36.

What is to be withdrawn
將 欲 歙 之

Must first be extended.
必 故 張 之

What is to be weakened
將 欲 弱 之

Must first be strengthened.
必 故 強 之

What is to be rejected
將 欲 廢 之

Must first be exalted.
必 故 興 之

What is to be taken
將 欲 取 之

Must first be given.
必 故 與 之

This is called subtle enlightenment:
是 謂 微 明

Gentle yielding conquers unyielding force.
柔 弱 勝 剛 強

As fish cannot be taken from the deep,
魚 不 可 脫 於 淵

So too the nation's greatest tools
國 之 利 器

Must not be offered to the people.
不 可 以 示 人

.37.

Dào never acts,
道 常 無 為

Yet nothing is left unaccomplished.
而 無 不 為

If lords and rulers abide with her,
侯 王 若 能 守 之

Then everything would be naturally transformed.
萬 物 將 自 化

They would be transformed, but desires arise in them,
化 而 欲 作

So I would restrain them
吾 將 鎮 之

By the natural simplicity of the nameless—
以 無 名 之 樸 [15]

And the natural simplicity of the nameless
無 名 之 樸

Settles things without desiring it.
夫 將 不 欲

Because she lacks nothing,
不欲

There is stillness;
以靜

The world settles itself.
天下將自正

Book II

THE BOOK OF VIRTUE

德經

.38.

The highest virtue lets go of virtue,
上 德 不 德

This is why it has virtue.
是 以 有 德

The lowest virtue never forgets virtue,
下 德 不 失 德

This is why it has no virtue.
是 以 無 德

The highest virtue does not act,
上 德 無 為

And does not interfere.
而 無 以 為

The lowest virtue acts
下 德 為 之

Only to manipulate things.
而 有 以 為

The highest kindness acts
上 仁[6] 為 之

And does not interfere;
而 無 以 為

The highest justice acts
上 義 為 之

Only to manipulate things.
而 有 以 為

The highest duty acts,
上 禮 為 之

But no one responds to it;
而 莫 之 應

So it stretches out its arms
則 攘 臂

And forces itself on them.
而 扔 之

Losing dào, still there is virtue.
故 失 道 而 後 德

Losing virtue, still there is kindness.
失 德 而 後 仁

Losing kindness, there is only unjust justice.
失 仁 而 後 義

Then after comes "duty."
失 義 而 後 禮

Duty is the husk of devotion—
夫 禮 者 忠 信 之 薄

The beginning of trouble.
而 亂 之 首

Superficial knowledge is the flower of dào—
前 識 者 道 之 華

The origin of foolishness.
而愚之始

Great ones reside in the substance,
是以大丈夫處其厚

Not dwelling in the husk.
不居其薄

Reside in the fruit,
處其實

Not dwelling in the flower.
不居其華

Reject the latter to receive the former.
故去彼取此

.39.

In ancient times, they attained unity:
昔 之 得 一 者

Heaven attained unity, and it became pure.
天 得 一 以 清

Earth attained unity, and it became peaceful.
地 得 一 以 寧

The spirits attained unity, and they became divine.
神 得 一 以 靈

The valleys attained unity and became full.
谷 得 一 以 盈

All things attained unity and began to grow.
萬 物 得 一 以 生

The rulers attained unity and ruled the world justly.
侯 王 得 一 以 為 天 下 正

This is what unity accomplishes.
其 致 之 也

When the heavens are not pure,
天 無 以 清

I fear they will split open.
將恐裂

When the earth is not peaceful,
地無以寧

I fear it will be shaken.
將恐廢

When the spirits are not divine,
神無以靈

I fear they will wither.
將恐歇

When the valleys are not full,
谷無以盈

I fear they will be exhausted.
將恐竭

When things cease to grow,
萬物無以生

I fear they will die.
將恐滅

When the rulers are not honorable,
侯 王 無 以 正

I fear their nations will be lost.
將 恐 蹶

The humble is the root of the valuable;
故 貴 以 賤 為 本

The lowly is the foundation of the high.
高 以 下 為 基

This is why the rulers call themselves
是 以 侯 王 自 稱

Solitary, desolate, and unworthy.
孤 寡 不 穀

Is this not taking the humble as the root?
此 非 以 賤 為 本

How scandalous this is!
邪 非 乎

The highest praise is not to be praised.
至 譽 無 譽

Do not desire things that shimmer like gems,
是 故 不 欲 琭 琭[28] 如 玉

But rather things that clatter like pebbles.
珞 珞 如 石

.40.

Cyclic returning is the motion of dào.
反[29] 者 道 之 動

Gentleness is dào's purpose.
弱 者 道 之 用 [10]

The world and everything in it grows from being,
天 下 萬 物 生 於 有

Being grows from non-being.
有 生 於 無

.41.

Great scholars hear dào
上 士 聞 道

And diligently follow her.
勤 而 行 之

Mediocre scholars hear dào;
中 士 聞 道

Sometimes following, sometimes losing their way.
若 存 若 亡

The inferior scholar hears dào
下 士 聞 道

And laughs heartily.
大 笑 之

If she were not laughable, she would not be dào.
不 笑 不 足 以 為 道

One could say that
故 建 言 有 之

Enlightened dào seems dark,
明 道 若 昧

Advancing in dào seems like retreating,
進 道 若 退

Smooth dào seems rough.
夷 道 若 纇

The highest virtue seems low,
上 德 若 谷

Abundant virtue seems lacking,
廣 德 若 不 足

Steadfast virtue seems unsteady.
建 德 若 偷

The substance of reality seems ethereal.
質 真 若 渝

Great whiteness seems sullied.
大 白 若 辱

A great square has no corners;
大 方 無 隅

A great tool works slowly.
大 器 晚 成

The greatest melody needs little accompaniment.
大 音 希 聲

The greatest image is invisible.
大 象 無 形

Dào is hidden and nameless,
道 隱 無 名

Yet dào alone skillfully provides and fulfills.
夫 唯 道 善 貸 且 成

.42.

Dào gives birth to the one.
道 生 一

One gives birth to two.
一 生 二

Two gives birth to three.
二 生 三

Three gives birth to all things.
三 生 萬 物

All things carry yin and embrace yang.
萬 物 負 陰 而 抱 陽

Blending their vital force, they achieve harmony.
沖 氣 [1] 以 為 和

Ugly-hearted people, orphans, and widows
人 之 所 惡 [2] 唯 孤 寡

Are considered worthless,
不 穀

Yet rulers call themselves by these titles.
而 王 公 以 為 稱

Things diminish, and then they increase;
故物或損之而益

People gain, and then they lose.
或益之而損

What others teach, I also teach:
人之所教我亦教之

Violent and aggressive people die miserably.
強梁者不得其死

This is the father of my teachings.
吾將以為教父

.43.

The softest thing in the world
天 下 之 至 柔

Surpasses the hardest thing in the world.
馳 騁 天 下 之 至 堅

Non-being penetrates that which has no crevices.
無 有 入 無 間

I know the benefit of non-action,
吾 是 以 知 無 為 之 有 益

But the benefit of non-action is a wordless teaching,
不 言 之 教 無 為 之 益

So the world seldom hears it.
天 下 希 及 之

.44.

Name or body, which is more intimate?
名 與 身 孰 親

Body or possessions, which is worth more?
身 與 貨 孰 多

Gain or loss, which is worse?
得 與 亡 孰 病

The stronger the attachment,
甚 愛

The more one is willing to waste.
必 大 費

More treasure
多 藏

Surely leads to more loss.
必 厚 亡

Know how to be content, and there is no dishonor.
故 知 足 不 辱

Know when to stop, and there is no danger.
知 止 不 殆

These are the ways to endure.
可 以 長 久

.45.

Great perfection seems imperfect,
大成若缺

But its purpose is never impaired.
其用[10]不弊

Great abundance seems empty,
大盈若沖

But its purpose never fails.
其用不窮

What is most straight seems twisted,
大直若屈

The greatest skill seems clumsy,
大巧若拙

The greatest eloquence seems awkward.
大辯若訥

Activity overcomes cold; stillness overcomes heat.
躁勝寒靜勝熱

Tranquil stillness can govern the world.
清靜為天下正

.46.

When the world follows dào,
天下有道

Galloping horses turn back to fertilize the fields.
卻走馬以糞

When the world is without dào,
天下無道

Warhorses breed in the countryside.
戎馬生於郊

There is no greater disaster
禍莫大於

Than not knowing how to be satisfied.
不知足

There is no greater misfortune than wanting more.
咎莫大於欲得

Knowing to be satisfied with satisfaction,
故知足之足

One is always satisfied!
常足矣

.47.

Without going out the door,
不 出 戶

One can know the whole world.
知 天 下

Without looking out of the window,
不 窺 牖

One can see the way of heaven.
見 天 道

The farther one goes,
其 出 彌 遠

The less one knows.
其 知 彌 少

The wise ones
是 以 聖 人

Know without going.
不 行 而 知

They do not look, yet they see.
不 見 而 明

They achieve without taking action.
不 為 而 成

.48.

Attending to learning accumulates day after day,
為學日益

Attending to dào diminishes day after day.
為道日損

Diminish, and continue to diminish,
損之又損

Until reaching the point of non-action.
以至於無為

No action is taken, but nothing is left undone.
無為而無不為

The world is united by never interfering.
取[26]天下常無事

As soon as one begins to interfere,
及其有事

One is unable to unite the world.
不足以取天下

.49.

The wise ones do not have hard hearts,
聖 人 常 無 心

So they let the people move their hearts.
以 百 姓 心 為 心[30]

The good ones, I treat well;
善 者 吾 善 之

The bad ones, I treat well,
不 善 者 吾 善 之

Because dào's virtue is good.
德[22] 善

With the sincere ones, I am sincere;
信 者 吾 信 之

With the insincere ones, I am sincere,
不 信 者 吾 信 之

Because dào's virtue is sincere.
德 信

The wise ones are in the midst of the world,
聖 人 在 天 下

Yet withdrawn, so withdrawn.
歙歙焉

To the world, they seem muddled and confused;
為天下渾其心

All the people eavesdrop and stare—
百姓皆注其耳目

The wise ones regard them all as children.
聖人皆孩之

.50.

Being born, we enter death.
出 生 入 死

Three out of ten are pursuers of life,
生 之 徒 十 有 三

Three out of ten are pursuers of death,
死 之 徒 十 有 三

Three out of ten hasten to death by clinging to life.
人 之 生 動 之 於 死 地 亦 十 有 三

Tell me, why is this?
夫 何 故

Because they worry themselves over life.
以 其 生 之 厚

I hear that those who live a good life,
蓋 聞 善 攝 生 者

While traveling in the hills,
路 行

Do not meet tigers or wild buffaloes.
不 遇 兕 虎

They do not enter the midst of battle,
入 軍

Nor wear armor or weapons;
不 被 甲 兵

A wild buffalo finds no place to put its horn;
兕 無 所 投 其 角

A tiger can find no place to sinks its claws;
虎 無 所 用 其 爪

Soldiers can find no place to thrust their blades.
兵 無 所 容 其 刃

Tell me, how is this possible?
夫 何 故

Because in them there is no place for death.
以 其 無 死 地

.51.

Dào produces them,
道 生 之

Dào's virtue cultivates them.
德[22] 畜 之

Matter shapes them,
物 形 之

Circumstances complete them.
勢 成 之

Everything without exception esteems dào
是 以 萬 物 莫 不 尊 道

And treasures dào's virtue.
而 貴 德

Dào's nobility
道 之 尊 也

And virtue's value
德 之 貴 也

Arise without anyone's order;
夫 莫 之 命

Always naturally so.
而常自然 [19]

Dào produces them,
故道生之

Dào's virtue cultivates them,
德畜之

Raises them, nurtures them,
長之育之

Covers them, matures them,
成之熟之

Rears them, protects them;
養之覆之

Grows them, but does not possess,
生而不有

Does her work, but expects no reward,
為而不恃

Leads, but does not control.
長而不宰

This is called dào's profound virtue.
是 謂 玄 德

.52.

The world has an origin,
天 下 有 始

Which may be called the world's mother.
以 為 天 下 母

When one's mother is known,
既 得 其 母

Then her children are known—
以 知 其 子

Then one returns to their mother,
復 守 其 母

And is always free of danger.
沒 身 不 殆

If one closes the mouth
塞 其 兌

And shuts the senses,
閉 其 門[31]

Until the end of life, one need not worry.
終 身 不 勤

If the mouth is opened,
開 其 兌

And affairs become overwhelming,
濟 其 事

Until the end of life, one is beyond rescue.
終 身 不 救

Perceiving the subtle is called enlightened.
見 小 曰 明

Abiding in gentleness is called strength.
守 柔 曰 強

Bask in her radiance,
用 其 光

Return to her enlightenment,
復 歸 其 明

And one will not be exposed to misfortune.
無 遺 身 殃

This is called bringing the eternal into time.
是 為 襲 常

.53.

If I suddenly attained wisdom,
使 我 介 然 有 知[32]

I would follow the great dào,
行 於 大 道

And straying would be my only fear.
唯 施 是 畏

Dào is very smooth,
大 道 甚 夷

But the people prefer rules and traditions.
而 人 好 徑

The palaces may be very splendid,
朝 甚 除

But the fields are filled with weeds,
田 甚 蕪

And the granaries are all but empty.
倉 甚 虛

They are clothed in elegant gowns,
服 文 采

Carrying sharp weapons,
帶 利 劍

Indulging in food and drink.
厭 飲 食

Having abundant wealth
財 貨 有 餘

Is but theft and vanity—
是 為 盜 夸

Alas, this is not dào!
非 道 也 哉

.54.

A good root cannot be uprooted;
善建者不拔

A good grip cannot be loosened—
善抱者不脫

To such a one, all will pay homage without ceasing.
子孫以祭祀不輟

Cultivate this in the self
修之於身

And dào's virtue will be abundant.
其德[22]乃真

Cultivate this in the home
修之於家

And dào's virtue will linger.
其德乃餘

Cultivate this in the village,
修之於鄉

And dào's virtue will be long-lasting.
其德乃長

Cultivate this in the nation,
修 之 於 邦

And dào's virtue will be teeming.
其 德 乃 丰

Cultivate this everywhere,
修 之 於 天 下

And dào's virtue will be all-pervasive.
其 德 乃 普

Consider the self as the self,
故 以 身 觀 身

The home as the home,
以 家 觀 家

The village as the village,
以 鄉 觀 鄉

The nation as the nation;
以 邦 觀 邦

See the world just as it is.
以 天 下 觀 天 下

How do I know things this way?
吾 何 以 知 天 下 然 哉

By stopping and sitting.
以 此 [21]

.55.

Those who keep the plenitude of dào's virtue
含 德 [22] 之 厚

Are like a newborn child:
比 於 赤 子

The serpent will not bite them,
毒 蟲 不 螫

Wild beasts will not attack them,
猛 獸 不 據

Birds of prey will not strike them.
攫 鳥 不 搏

Their bones, yielding,
骨 弱

Their muscles, pliant,
筋 柔

Yet their grasp is firm.
而 握 固

They have not yet known sexual union,
未 知 牝 牡 之 合

Yet they are fully aroused.
而峻作

They are brimming with potential.
精之至也

All day they cry, yet never become hoarse.
終日號而不嗄

They are brimming with tranquility.
和之至也

Knowing tranquility
知和

Is called the unchanging.
曰常

Knowing the unchanging
知常

Is called enlightenment.
曰明

Having fullness of life
益生

Is called a blessing.
日祥

Directing the vital force with the mind
心使氣 [11]

Is called strength.
日強

Overgrown creatures will grow old,
物壯則老

This is called going against dào.
謂之不道

Going against dào leads to an early end.
不道早已

.56.

Those who are wise do not speak;
知 者 不 言

Those who speak are not wise;
言 者 不 知 [32]

Close the mouth,
塞 其 兌

Shut the senses,
閉 其 門 [31]

Blunt sharpened tongues,
挫 其 銳

And end disputes.
解 其 紛

Humble the exalted,
和 其 光

Unite the people—
同 其 塵 [33]

This is called the mystery of union,
是 謂 玄 同

This causes one to become impossible to approach,
故 不 可 得

Yet impossible to avoid;
而 親 不 可 得 而 疏

Impossible to benefit,
不 可 得

Yet impossible to harm;
而 利 不 可 得 而 害

Impossible to esteem,
不 可 得

Yet impossible to disgrace;
而 貴 不 可 得 而 賤

This is the greatest treasure of the world.
故 為 天 下 貴

.57.

A nation is governed by rules,
以 正 治 國

A war is won by lawlessness,
以 奇 用 兵

The whole world is united when meddling ceases.
以 無 事 取 [26] 天 下

How do I know it is so?
吾 何 以 知 其 然 哉

By stopping and sitting, I see:
以 此 [21]

The more restrictions and taboos in the world,
天 下 多 忌 諱

The poorer the people.
而 民 彌 貧

The sharper the people's weapons,
人 多 利 器

The more disordered the nation.
國 家 滋 昏

The more clever and cunning the people,
人 多 伎 巧

The more trickery will occur.
奇 物 滋 起

The more rules and commands are promulgated,
法 令 滋 彰

The more thieves and robbers appear.
盜 賊 多 有

The wise ones say:
故 聖 人 云

I am without action,
我 無 為

So the people reform themselves.
而 民 自 化

I provide room for stillness,
我 好 靜

So the people adjust themselves.
而 民 自 正

I do not interfere,
我 無 事

So the people enrich themselves.
而 民 自 富

I have no attachments,
我 無 欲

So the people return to natural simplicity.
而 民 自 樸 [15]

.58.

When government is subdued, subdued,
其 政 悶 悶

The people are pure, pure.
其 民 淳 淳

When government is prying, prying,
其 政 察 察

The people are restless, restless.
其 民 缺 缺

Good fortune rests upon misery,
禍 兮 福 之 所 倚

And misery is concealed in good fortune.
福 兮 禍 之 所 伏

Who knows where it ends?
孰 知 其 極

The world is unjust,
其 無 正 也

But justice turns to injustice,
正 復 為 奇

123

And good turns to misfortune.
善 復 為 妖

Every day, society's confusion endures.
人 之 迷 其 日 固 久

The wise ones are sharp,
是 以 聖 人 方

But do not cut.
而 不 割

Acute, but not piercing.
廉 而 不 劌

Direct, but not severe.
直 而 不 肆

Brilliant, but not blinding.
光 而 不 耀

.59.

To care for humanity and serve heaven,
治 人 事 天

Nothing surpasses prudence.
莫 若 嗇

Only through prudence
夫 唯 嗇

May one be prepared.
是 謂 早 服

By being prepared,
早 服 謂 之

Dào's virtue is abundant.
重 積 德 [22]

An abundance of virtue
重 積 德

Means nothing is impossible.
則 無 不 克

Because nothing is impossible,
無 不 克

There are no known limits.
則莫知其極

Because there are no known limits,
莫知其極

One is then able to maintain the nation.
可以有國

One who maintains the mother of the nation
有國之母

Can endure.
可以長久

This is called having deep roots and a sturdy trunk;
是謂深根固柢

The dào of ever-increasing insight
長生久視之道

.60.

Governing a great nation is like frying a small fish.
治 大 國 若 烹 小 鮮

Govern the world with dào,
以 道 涖 天 下

And the dark spirits will not have power.
其 鬼 不 神

The dark spirits will not have power,
非 其 鬼 不 神

And their power will not harm the people.
其 神 不 傷 人

Their power will not harm the people,
非 其 神 不 傷 人

And the wise ones will not harm the people.
聖 人 亦 不 傷 人

Neither of them will cause harm;
夫 兩 不 相 傷

And so their virtue unites and returns.
故 德 交 歸 焉

.61.

A great nation, flowing down the world's stream,
大 國 者 下 流 天 下 之

Is a confluence of the world's feminine energy.
交 天 下 之 牝 也

The feminine, through her stillness,
牝 常 以 靜

Always overcomes the masculine.
勝 牡

By stillness,
以 靜

She strikes at the root.
為 下

If a great nation defers to a small nation,
故 大 國 以 下 小 國

Then it can unite the small nation.
則 取[26] 小 國

If a small nation defers to a great nation,
小 國 以 下 大 國

Then it unites with the great nation.
則 取 於 大 國

Some unite by deferring,
故 或 下 以 取

And others are united by deferring.
或 下 而 取

A great nation only wants to annex and herd people.
大 國 不 過 欲 兼 畜 人

A small nation only wants to serve its people.
小 國 不 過 欲 入 事 人

Each of them obtains that which they desire,
夫 兩 者 各 得 所 欲

But it behooves the great to defer to the small.
大 者 宜 為 下

.62.

Dào is the silent reservoir of all things—
道 者 萬 物 之 奧[34]

The treasure of the good person,
善 人 之 寶

The guardian of the bad.
不 善 人 之 所 保

Beautiful words earn respect;
美 言 可 以 市 尊

Noble actions confer honor.
美 行 可 以 加 人

Why shun people for their faults?
人 之 不 善 何 棄 之 有

When the emperor is crowned
故 立 天 子

And his three ministers are appointed,
置 三 公

Though he may have precious jade
雖 有 拱 璧

And be preceded by four horses,
以先馳馬

He is not superior to one who sits and offers dào.
不如坐進此[21]道

This is the reason that the ancients treasured dào.
古之所以貴此道者何也

Through her they obtained what they sought
不曰求以得

And were forgiven their transgressions.
有罪以免邪

This is why the whole world treasures her.
故為天下貴

.63.

Act without action,
為 無 為

Do without doing,
事 無 事

Find flavor even in what is flavorless.
味 無 味

Whether great or small, many or few,
大 小 多 少

Respond to injuries with virtue.
報 怨 以 德

Deal with the difficult while it is still easy.
圖 難 於 其 易

Deal with the great while it is still small.
為 大 於 其 細

The world's difficulties
天 下 難 事

Always arise as simple things.
必 作 於 易

The world's great affairs
天 下 大 事

Always arise as small things.
必 作 於 細

The wise ones
是 以 聖 人

Do not strive after great things;
終 不 為 大

This is why their accomplishments are great.
故 能 成 其 大

Frivolous commitments are divorced from trust.
夫 輕 諾 必 寡 信

Over-simplicity leads to great difficulties.
多 易 必 多 難

The wise ones confront difficult things;
是 以 聖 人 猶 難 之

And so there is never difficulty!
故 終 無 難 矣

.64.

What is at rest is easily grasped.
其 安 易 持

What has not yet happened is easily prepared for.
其 未 兆 易 謀

What is fragile is easily broken.
其 脆 易 泮

What is small is easily scattered.
其 微 易 散

Take action before it emerges,
為 之 於 未 有

Govern before there is trouble.
治 之 於 未 亂

A tree as big as one's embrace
合 抱 之 木

Grows from a tiny seed.
生 於 毫 末

A nine story tower
九 層 之 台

Begins with a heap of earth.
起於累土

A long journey
千里之行

Begins where one's feet stand.
始於足下

Taking action is failure;
為者敗之

Taking hold lets it slip—
執者失之

The wise ones do not act,
聖人無為

So that there is no failure.
故無敗

They do not take hold,
無執

So that it does not slip.
故無失

The people follow their affairs,
民之從事

Constantly approaching success,
常於幾成

Yet failing.
而敗之

As patient in the end as the beginning,
慎終如始

There will be no failure.
則無敗事

The wise ones
是以聖人

Desire to be desireless,
欲不欲

And do not esteem treasures obtained with difficulty.
不貴難得之貨

They learn to be unlearned,
學不學

And return to where the people have overshot.
復 眾 人 之 所 過

They support the spontaneous nature of all things
以 輔 萬 物 之 自 然 [19]

Without daring to act.
而 不 敢 為

.65.

The ancient ones practiced dào well;
古 之 善 為 道 者

They did not seek to enlighten the people,
非 以 明 民

But let them follow their own simplicity.
將 以 愚 之

The people are impossible to govern
民 之 難 治

Because of their cleverness.
以 其 智 多

To rule the nation cleverly
故 以 智 治 國

Is the nation's ruin.
國 之 賊

To rule the nation without cleverness
不 以 智 治 國

Is the nation's good fortune.
國 之 福

Knowing this balance
知 此 兩

Is knowing the rule of heaven.
者 亦 稽 式

Never forgetting this standard
常 知 稽 式

Is called profound virtue.
是 謂 玄 德

Profound virtue goes deep and distant!
玄 德 深 矣 遠 矣

It returns things to their source!
與 物 反 矣

Then greatest harmony is attained.
然 後 乃 至 大 順

.66.

The reason that the rivers and seas
江 海 之 所 以

Can become the rulers of the valleys
能 為 百 谷 王 者

Is because they are good at staying in low places.
以 其 善 下 之

This is why they can be the rulers of the valleys.
故 能 為 百 谷 王

The wise ones speak humbly to the people,
是 以 聖 人 欲 上 民

And do not speak down to them.
必 以 言 下 之

One who wishes to lead others
欲 先 民

Must leave their assumptions behind.
必 以 身 後 之

The wise ones dwell in high places
是 以 聖 人 處 上

But the people do not feel their weight.
而民不重

They stand in front without obstructing the people—
處前而民不害

This is why
是以

The world never tires of joyously exalting them.
天下樂推而不厭

Because they do not strive against nature,
以其不爭 [3]

Nothing in the world can strive against them.
故天下莫能與之爭

.67.

All say that
天 下 皆 謂

Dào is great,
我 道 大

Great, and resembling nothing else.
大 而 不 肖

It is precisely because she resembles nothing else
夫 唯 不 肖

That she can be great.
故 似 大

If she resembled others, she would be trivial.
若 肖 久 矣 其 細 也 夫

I have three treasures that I hold and cherish:
我 有 三 寶 持 而 保 之

One is called compassion.
一 曰 慈

The second is called moderation.
二 曰 儉

The third is called not daring to be the world's leader.
三曰不敢為天下先

Compassion begets the ability to be without fear.
慈故能勇

Moderation begets the ability to be generous.
儉故能廣

Not daring to be the world's leader
不敢為天下先

Allows one's talents to endure.
故能成器長

Seeking bravery without compassion,
今舍慈且勇

Seeking generosity without moderation,
舍儉且廣

Seeking leadership without humility,
舍後且先

These things are fatal!
死矣

Only compassion can bring victory out of a battle—
夫 慈 以 戰 則 勝

If one is guarded in this way,
以 守

They become impregnable.
則 固

Heaven will come to save those
天 將 救 之

Who are guarded by compassion.
以 慈 衛 之

.68.

A well-trained commander does not make war.
善為士者不武

A well-fought battle is not violent.
善戰者不怒

A skillful conquerer does not compete.
善勝敵者不爭

A good leader is humble.
善用人者為之下

This is called the virtue of not striving against nature.
是謂不爭³之德

This is called the strength to cooperate with others.
是謂用人之力

This is called the sublime union with heaven.
是謂配天

The supreme ultimate of the ancient ones.
古之極也

.69.

In military engagements, there is a saying:
用 兵 有 言

I do not dare act as a ruler,
吾 不 敢 為 主

But act as a guest.
而 為 客

Nor dare to advance an inch
不 敢 進 寸

Without retreating a foot.
而 退 尺

This is called movement without moving,
是 謂 行 無 行

Reaching out without forcing,
攘 無 臂

Confronting without attacking,
扔 無 敵

Seizing without soldiers.
執 無 兵

There is no greater calamity
禍莫大

Than making light of one's opponent.
於輕敵

Making light of one's opponent
輕敵

Risks destroying my treasures.
幾喪吾寶

When soldiers meet in battle,
故抗兵相若

The reluctant one will prevail.
哀者勝矣

.70.

My words are very easy to understand
吾 言 甚 易 知

And very easy to practice.
甚 易 行

But no one is able to understand them
天 下 莫 能 知

Or practice them
莫 能 行

My words have an ancestor,
言 有 宗

My deeds have a master,
事 有 君

It is precisely because she is unknown
夫 唯 無 知

That my teachings are unknown.
是 以 不 我 知

Those who know my teachings are a rare sight,
知 我 者 希

For the wise ones wear coarse clothes
是以聖人被褐

To hide their treasures.
而懷玉

.71.

To know that one does not know is noble.
知 不 知 尚

Not knowing yet thinking one knows is a sickness.
不 知 知 病

The wise ones are not sick.
聖 人 不 病

Because they are sick of this sickness,
以 其 病 病

They are not sick.
是 以 不 病

.72.

When the people are not afraid of harm,
民 不 畏 威

They will be greatly harmed.
則 大 威 至

Do not restrict the people's lives,
無 狎 其 所 居

Do not oppress their livelihood.
無 厭 其 所 生

It is only because someone oppresses
夫 唯 不 厭

That there is oppression.
是 以 不 厭

This is why the wise ones know themselves
是 以 聖 人 自 知

But do not to parade themselves about.
不 自 見

Love yourself, but do not treasure yourself.
自 愛 不 自 貴

.73.

He who shows bravery by taking risks will die.
勇 於 敢 則 殺

He who shows bravery by not taking risks will live.
勇 於 不 敢 則 活

Some things benefit, while others harm.
此 兩 者 或 利 或 害

Who knows why heaven despises what it despises?
天 之 所 惡 孰 知 其 故

Even the wise ones consider this question difficult.
是 以 聖 人 猶 難 之

The dào of heaven
天 之 道

Does not strive, yet deftly conquers.
不 爭 而 善 勝

She does not speak, yet skillfully responds.
不 言 而 善 應

She does not ask, yet she receives.
不 召 而 自 來

She has no aim, yet her planning is impeccable.
繟 然 而 善 謀

The holes in heaven's net are vast and wide,
天 網 恢 恢

Yet nothing slips through.
疏 而 不 失

.74.

The people do not fear death,
民 不 畏 死

So how can executions threaten them?
奈 何 以 死 懼 之

But if the people fear death,
若 使 民 常 畏 死

Then they become vicious,
而 為 奇 者

Then who would dare arrest and execute them?
吾 得 執 而 殺 之 孰 敢

There is already a natural death to do the killing.
常 有 司 殺 者 殺

One who kills in the stead of natural death
夫 代 司 殺 者 殺

Is cutting wood for a master carpenter.
是 謂 代 大 匠 斲

One who cuts wood for a master carpenter
夫 代 大 匠 斲 者

Seldom remains uninjured by their own hands!
希 有 不 傷 其 手 矣

.75.

The people are starving
民 之 飢

Because their rulers feast on their taxes.
以 其 上 食 稅 之 多

This is why they are starving.
是 以 飢

The people are difficult to rule
民 之 難 治

Because their rulers are meddlesome.
以 其 上 之 有 為

This is why they are difficult to rule.
是 以 難 治

The people take death lightly
民 之 輕 死

Because their rulers make much of life.
以 其 上 求 生 之 厚

This is why they take death lightly.
是 以 輕 死

Only one who does not strive for life
夫 唯 無 以 生 為 者

Has a life worth honoring.
是 賢 於 貴 生

.76.

While they grow, people are
人 之 生 也

Tender and fragile.
柔 弱

When they die, they are
其 死 也

Rigid and stiff.
堅 強

While they grow, the grass and trees are
草 木 之 生 也

Yielding and delicate.
柔 脆

When they die, they are
其 死 也

Brittle and rotten.
枯 槁

Rigidity and stiffness pursue death;
故 堅 強 者 死 之 徒

Tenderness and fragility pursue life;
柔弱者生之徒

This is why unyielding soldiers cannot win.
是以兵強則滅

An unyielding tree will meet the axe.
木強則折

The unyielding are toppled from their places.
強大處下

The tender and fragile will be lifted up.
柔弱處上

.77.

Heaven's way
天 之 道

Is like drawing a bow:
其 猶 張 弓 歟

The top is pulled down
高 者 抑 之

As the bottom is lifted.
下 者 舉 之

The long is diminished
有 餘 者 損 之

The short is supplemented.
不 足 者 補 之

The dào of heaven diminishes whatever is abundant
天 之 道 損 有 餘

And supplements what is lacking.
而 補 不 足

The way of society is not so:
人 之 道 則 不 然

It diminishes the lacking,
損不足

And adds to what is already abundant.
以奉有餘

Who can take the surplus
孰能有餘

And offer it to the world?
以奉天下

Only those who follow dào.
唯有道者

The wise ones do their work, expecting no reward.
是以聖人為而不恃

Merit success without taking credit,
功成而不處

They do not act in order to display their excellence.
其不欲見賢

.78.

Nothing is as tender and weak as water,
天 下 莫 柔 弱 於 水

Yet even the most forceful attack
而 攻 堅 強 者

Cannot conquer it.
莫 之 能 勝

For this reason, nothing can replace it.
其 無 以 易 之

The weak surpasses unyielding force,
弱 之 勝 強

Tenderness surpasses aggression.
柔 之 勝 剛

This is not unknown to the world,
天 下 莫 不 知

Yet none can practice it.
莫 能 行

The wise ones say:
是 以 聖 人 云

One who takes on the nation's shame
受國之垢

Is called the ruler of the land.
是謂社稷主

One who takes on the nation's misfortunes
受國不祥

Is called the ruler of the world.
是為天下王

True words seem paradoxical.
正言若反

.79.

Make peace with enemies,
和大怨

And yet hatred still remains.
必有餘怨

How can this be any good?
安可以為善

The wise ones meet their obligations
是以聖人執左契[35]

Without blaming others;
而不責於人

The virtuous ones merely keep contracts;
有德司契

Those without virtue hold others responsible.
無德司徹

Heaven's way is without preference,
天道無親

Yet is always on the side of the good.
常與善人

.80.

A small nation with few citizens;
小 國 寡 民

Even if they possess ten times one hundred tools,
使 有 什 伯 之 器

They do not use them.
而 不 用

If the people take death seriously,
使 民 重 死

They will not travel far.
而 不 遠 徙

Although they possess boats and carriages,
雖 有 舟 輿

They find no place to ride them.
無 所 乘 之

Though they possess weapons,
雖 有 甲 兵

They do not display them.
無 所 陳 之

Let the people return to knotting cords
使 民 復 結 繩

To keep their accounts.
而 用 之 [36]

They enjoy their food,
甘 其 食

Their clothes are beautiful,
美 其 服

They are content with their homes.
安 其 居

They find joy in everyday life.
樂 其 俗

Neighboring communities can see one another,
鄰 國 相 望

Roosters and dogs can be heard between them,
雞 犬 之 聲 相 聞

Yet the people will grow old and die,
民 至 老 死

Never having visited them.
不 相 往 來

.81.

Sincere words are not beautiful—
信 言 不 美

Beautiful words are not sincere.
美 言 不 信

The good do not argue—
善 者 不 辯

Arguments are not good.
辯 者 不 善

Wisdom is not learned—
知 [32] 者 不 博

Learning is not wisdom.
博 者 不 知

The wise ones do not hoard.
聖 人 不 積

The more they act for others,
既 以 為 人

The more they have.
己 愈 有

The more they share with the people,
既 以 與 人

The more they receive.
己 愈 多

Heaven's way benefits
天 之 道 利

And does not injure.
而 不 害

The wise one's way
聖 人 之 道

Is to act without striving against nature.
為 而 不 爭 [3]

NOTES

1 In Verse 1, The character 欲 is made up of the character for "lack" and the character "valley." I have translated this line unconventionally based on the frequent usage of "valley" as a metaphor for dào. While I have maintained a more orthodox approach to other instances of this character, they could certainly be read in this sense as well.

2 The character 惡 may be translated "hateful," "ugly," "despised," "evil," and so on. Etymologically, it consists of the character for heart and a radical that here means "deformed." Thus, "ugly-hearted," used in Verses 2 and 42.

3 The character 爭 may simply be translated "to strive." In spaces when it seems to amplify the text (Verses 8, 22, 56, 66, 68, 81), I have translated it "to strive against nature." This is because it not only captures the spirit of the *Dàodéjīng*, but also because the character itself is an image of an animal's claw and a human hand fighting over a stick—a perfect image of the battle between humanity and nature.

4 The character 知 is used in various senses throughout the text; it generally means "knowledge." In Verses 3 as well as in 10, it is used in a negative sense, so I have chosen to translate it the same way as 學, "learnedness," which is used exclusively in the negative throughout. (*see also* note 32.)

5 In Verse 4, the literal translation of this line would be "image-lord's origin." This has been translated variously as the origin of gods, the origin of nature, etc. (Though the character 象, usually translated "image," may also be interpreted "seems to be.") I have chosen to interpret the "image-lord" as being akin to the Jungian concept of "archetype," but I readily admit that this line is difficult, and any translation, including my own, will be lacking.

6 Paradoxically, the character 仁, which might be translated "kindness" or "humanity," is sometimes used in the positive sense (Verse 8), sometimes in a neutral sense (Verse 38), and, most often, in a negative sense (Verses 5, 18, 19.) In the negative sense, it seems to indicate partiality or kindness done out of duty rather than care. I have translated it differently in each context to reflect this.

NOTES

7 In Verse 5, the literal translation of this line is "like straw dogs." I have chosen to capture its meaning in the word "impartially" and leave researching the cultural significance of "straw dogs" as an exercise for the reader.

8 In Verse 6, the character 牝 means "female," but also "valley" or even "keyhole." I have used "womb" to try to capture the various meanings.

9 In the text, there are several places where a character is duplicated to place emphasis, and in most of these instances I have retained the duplication in the translation in order to capture the feel of the original. In Verse 6 I deviate from this and translate 系系 as "saturating everything," because "saturating, saturating" would be an awkward and confusing rendering. (*see also* note 28.)

10 The character 用 is most easily translated "to use," "to employ," or possibly "to enjoy." In some places such translation is limiting due to the utilitarian baggage of the English word, and in several chapters (Verses 6, 11, 40, 45) I have chosen to interpret it in the sense of "realizing the purpose of."

11 The character 氣, transliterated *qì*, is a complex concept in Chinese philosophy, and demands significant research for a passable understanding, which I leave as an exercise for the reader. It appears in Verses 10, 42, and 55, and I have translated it "vital force" for lack of a better alternative.

12 In Verse 10, the literal translation of 天門開闔 is "heaven's gate opens and closes." The "gate of heaven" refers to the senses, and I have chosen to make this meaning explicit in my translation. (*see also* note 31.)

13 The literal translation of this line in Verse 10 might be "It is possible to be feminine!" My translation is based on the particular character 雌, conventionally meaning "female." The right portion of the character means "bird," while the left means "this." The character for "this," 此, is used several times in the text to imply a meditative stance (Verses 21, 54, 62; *see also* note 20), thus "tranquil." To preserve the feminine implications of the character as well as the dào's characterization as "mother," I have used the phrase "mother bird." While this is certainly not the most literal

translation, I find the imagery of a bird patiently incubating her eggs to capture the meaning well.

14 In Verse 13, the character 身 may mean "body" or "self." Because the meaning is ambiguous here, I have tried to capture both. By "unchangeable identity," I mean to capture a sense of ego that is, like the body, effete and material, which we attempt to maintain at all costs. This seems to capture the meaning of the text.

15 The character 樸 means "simple" or "genuine." It is often translated "uncarved block" due to the character's etymology. I have chosen to translate it "natural simplicity" to capture the meaning of the character as well as its etymological connection to the undomesticated wilderness. (*see* Verses 15, 19, 28, 32, 37, 57.)

16 The character 複, like 反, means "return," but here in Verse 16 it is meant to imply a sort of eternal return—a cycle—much like 反 is employed in Verse 40 (*see* note 29.)

17 This line of Verse 16 might be translated "drown the self, be free of danger," or "give up the self, be free of danger," or any other number of ways. The general sense seems to be freeing one's self from danger by exposing one's "self" to danger.

18 This line of Verse 17 might be translated "So quietly he treasures words," but the character 其 can also indicate a question, and so I have chosen my translation accordingly, which I believe better captures the sense of a silent ruler.

19 The phrase 自然 is an important technical term in dàoism, and might be translated "self-so." It may be said to mean that which genuinely honors the nature that formed it, and I have translated it somewhat differently in each place that it occurs (Verses 17, 23, 25, 51, 64) to reflect that meaning in each context.

20 The character 聖 usually means "wise" or "sacred," but in Verse 19, where it is used in a negative sense, I have rendered it "self-righteousness" to indicate the artifice of wisdom.

21 The character 此 generally means "this." The component on the left of the character means "stop" while that on the right depicts a seated figure. Hence my choice to amplify the meaning

NOTES

as it appears in Verses 21, 54, 57, and 62.

22 I have translated 德, as "dào's virtue" in several places (Verses 23, 28, 49, 51, 54, 55, 59.) This is in accord with the meaning of the character explicated in Verse 21, which tells us that 德 can only come from dào.

23 In Verse 26, the character 重, meaning "baggage," is the same character used earlier to mean "heavy." This constitutes a pun that is lost in the translation.

24 More literally, this line in Verse 27 might read "This demands awe," but I have chosen a translation that amplifies its reference to failing to "value their teacher" and "love their lesson."

25 In Verse 28, the character 制 means "system," "establishment," or "power." It consists of an image of a large tree being cut down. This is the reverse of the character 樸, which literally means "uncarved block of wood," and is translated in this passage as "nature's simplicity" (*see* note 15.) In this line, the 制 is described as "uncut." Literally, perhaps, it claims that "the cut wood remains uncut." Because this refers back to "nature's simplicity," I have chosen to translate it in a way that reflects all of these concerns, along with the claim that the wise ones "gather the pieces."

26 The character 取 generally means "to take hold" or "to receive," but in several places the more context-appropriate meaning is "to bring together" or "to unite" (Verses 29, 48, 57, 61.)

27 In Verse 35, the character 用 is interpreted to mean realizing the purpose of dào, which in this context is providence. (*see* note 10.)

28 In the text, there are several places where a character is duplicated to place emphasis, and in most of these instances I have retained the duplication in the translation in order to capture the feel of the original. In Verse 39 I deviate from this and translate 琭琭 as "things that shimmer," because "jade, jade" would be an awkward and confusing rendering. In the following line, I have followed a similar convention. (*see also* note 9.)

173

NOTES

29 The character 反, like 複, means "return," but here in Verse 40 it is meant to imply a sort of eternal return—a cycle—much like 複 is employed in Verse 16 (*see* note 16.)

30 Many translations have these opening lines of Verse 49 claim something about the wise ones taking the people's mind as their own. Because the verse is specifically about the wise ones reacting differently than those who act upon them, this seems inappropriate. Instead, these lines appear to say that the wise ones' hearts are moved by the people—that they care for the people rather than simply reacting in kind.

31 The phrase 閉其門 found in Verses 52 and 56 literally means "shut the gates," but is being used as a metaphor for the senses. I believe my translation amplifies the meaning as well as bringing it into congruence with the line preceding it. (*see also* note 12.)

32 The character 知 is used in various senses throughout the text. While it generally means "knowledge," it seems to indicate something deeper in Verses 53, 56 and 81. I have chosen to translate it "wisdom." (*see also* note 4)

33 In Verse 56, the phrase 挫其銳解其紛和其光同其塵 may be more literally translated "blunt the sharp, loosen the knots, soften the lights, unite the scattered dust." The translation presented is meant to amplify the metaphor that is being presented.

34 In Verse 62, the character 奧 may mean "obscure," "profound," "container," or "storehouse." It originally referred to the southwest corner of a house, where treasure is kept. The character is made of a "treasure" inside of a container, above the character for "great." To maintain the sense of profundity, its role as a container, and the frequent allusions to water metaphors in the text, I have interpolated the translation "silent reservoir."

35 In Verse 79, the line 聖人執左契 may be more literally translated "The wise ones keep the left contract." The cultural significance of this is that the wise one repays their debts. I have chosen to translate this more generally as meeting obligations.

36 In Verse 80, this line literally means "and using them." The use of knotting cords is to keep track of information, usually

numbers—the practice resulted eventually in the abacus. My translation is meant to reflect this meaning.

Made in the USA
Monee, IL
29 March 2021